Crazy Planes

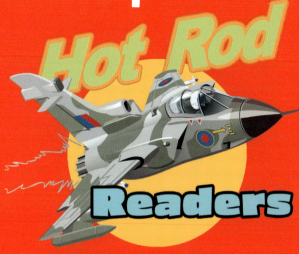

Craig A. Lopetz

TABLE OF CONTENTS

What Are Crazy Planes?	2
Glossary	23
Index	23

A Crabtree Seedlings Book

What Are Crazy Planes?

Crazy planes are **artist** drawings.

Some are drawn with **airbrush** paints.

Some are drawn on a computer.

Crazy planes come in many sizes and colors.

They take us where we want to go.

Most crazy planes have propellers.

propellers spin around and move air

Some have jet **engines**. They go super fast.

Some crazy planes help protect us.

There are old crazy planes.

And there are really, really old crazy planes.

There are big crazy planes that carry lots of people.

There are giant crazy planes that carry lots of **cargo**.

Most planes have one pair of wings.

one pair

Some have two pairs of wings!

two pairs

Real Planes and Crazy Planes

C-17 Globemaster

Sukhoi Su-27

Beechcraft King Air

22

Glossary

airbrush (AIR-brush): An airbrush is a tool that sprays paint.

artist (AR-tist): An artist is someone who is very good at drawing, painting, or making things.

cargo (KAR-go): Cargo is goods carried by a ship or a plane.

engines (EN-jinz): Engines are machines that give vehicles and aircraft power.

Index

artist   2
engines   8
people   17
propellers   6
wings   20, 21

School-to-Home Support for Caregivers and Teachers

This book helps children grow by letting them practice reading. Here are a few guiding questions to help the reader build his or her comprehension skills. Possible answers appear here in red.

Before Reading
- **What do I think this book is about?** I think this book is about crazy planes. I think this book is about how to draw crazy looking planes.
- **What do I want to learn about this topic?** I want to learn how I can draw crazy planes. I want to learn about the parts on a plane.

During Reading
- **I wonder why...** I wonder why most crazy planes have propellers. I wonder why some planes have only one pair of wings and others have two pairs of wings.

- **What have I learned so far?** I have learned that propellers on planes spin around fast and move air. I have learned that engines are machines that give vehicles and airplanes power.

After Reading
- **What details did I learn about this topic?** I have learned that crazy planes can be drawn with an airbrush or on a computer. I have learned that some crazy planes have jet engines and can go super fast.
- **Read the book again and look for the glossary words.** I see the word *engines* on page 8, and the word *cargo* on page 18. The other glossary words are found on page 22.

Library and Archives Canada Cataloguing in Publication

CIP available at Library and Archives Canada

Library of Congress Cataloging-in-Publication Data

CIP available at Library of Congress

Crabtree Publishing Company
www.crabtreebooks.com   1-800-387-7650

Written by: Craig A. Lopetz
Print coordinator: Katherine Berti

Print book version produced jointly with Blue Door Education in 2023

Printed in the U.S.A./072022/CG20220201

Content produced and published by Blue Door Education, Melbourne Beach FL USA. This title Copyright Blue Door Education. All rights reserved. No part of this book may be reproduced or utilized in any form or by any means, electronic or mechanical including photocopying, recording, or by any information storage and retrieval system without permission in writing from the publisher.

PHOTO CREDITS:
Special thanks to Mechanic for the great art. Cover: shutterstock.com | ©Mechanik. Pages 2-22 :shutterstock.com | Mechanik, Page 4-5: ©shutterstock.com/ ChonnieArtwork. Page 6-7: ©shutterstock.com/ MarySan. Page 8-9: ©shutterstock.com/ klyaksun. ©shutterstock.com/ Quality Stock Arts. ©shutterstock.com/ nazlisart (flag). Page 12-13: ©shutterstock.com/ Petr Vaclavek. Page 14-15: ©shutterstock.com/ one AND only. Page 16-17: ©shutterstock.com/ Chockdee Permploysiri. Page 18-19: ©shutterstock.com/ Oleksiy Mark. Page 20-21: ©shutterstock.com/ DropOfWax. Page 22: ©shutterstock.com/ Soos Jozsef. ©shutterstock.com/ InsectWorld. ©shutterstock.com/ SpaceKris. shutterstock.com/Mechanik.

Published in the United States
Crabtree Publishing
347 Fifth Ave.
Suite 1402-145
New York, NY 10016

Published in Canada
Crabtree Publishing
616 Welland Ave.
St. Catharines, Ontario
L2M 5V6